DREAMS

RECORD & INTERPRET YOUR MESSAGES FROM GOD

DREAMS: RECORD & INTERPRET YOUR MESSAGES FROM GOD

ISBN: 978-1-9999616-7-1

First published in the UK by Pura Track Publishing in April 2020.

For business enquiries, email: questions@toremathompson.uk

All scripture quotations are taken from the King James version of the Holy Bible.

A NOTE FROM THE AUTHOR

Dreams from God are a gift.

The voice of the Lord is multifaceted, and dreams are one of the ways in which He chooses to speak to us.

To understand our dreams, we must understand the language of the Spirit of God; He speaks in pictures and symbols, and never contradicts the Holy Scriptures.

At times, the meaning of a dream may seem obvious upon waking up; however, more often than not, Abba (Father) requires us to seek Him in order to gain a deeper understanding of what He is saying.

It is the glory of God to conceal a thing:
but the honour of kings is to search out a matter.
(Proverbs 25:2)

Dreams are an invitation from God to know Him more, to gain His heart, to discover our destiny, to learn and grow in Him.

As much as it is an honour that God would choose to speak to us through the intimate vehicle of dreams, the greater honour is to learn to **understand** the voice of the Lord when He speaks.

Understanding the voice of God begins with having a good grounding in Scripture—you need His Word *in you*—there is no substitute for this. The Bible is the plumb line, helping you to discern whether your dream is from God, the enemy or self.

With this foundation in place, you must learn to understand the **unique** way the Lord speaks to *you*. Yes, there are biblical principles and general symbols that are standard across the board; however, your relationship with the Father is unique, and He will speak to you in a way that only *you* are designed to understand. Abba has a way in which He has designed *you* to know Him; therefore, He will speak to you accordingly.

Dreams from God are a gift. Let us be good stewards of our dreams by recording that which He gives us. Let us also be diligent to learn to sit before Him so that we might gain an understanding of what He is saying.

Amen.

And He said, Hear now My words:
If there be a prophet among you,
I the LORD will make Myself known unto him in a vision,
and will speak unto him in a **dream**.
(NUMBERS 12:6)

RECORD YOUR DREAM

DATE:

TIME:

INTERPRETATION

Was this dream from God? ☐ Yes ☐ No

(If the dream was not from God, it does not require an interpretation. However, still sit with the Lord to identify the source and to see what He would have you do.)

RECORD KEY SYMBOLS

COLOURS / SHADES / SHAPES / NUMBERS
NAMES / PEOPLE / BODY PARTS / CHARACTERISTICS
PLACES / TIMES / DATES / POSITIONS
THOUGHTS / FEELINGS / SOUNDS / SMELLS
OBJECTS / ACTIONS / ANIMALS / VEHICLES / FOOD

RECORD UNDERSTANDING

WHAT GOD IS SAYING...
KEY SCRIPTURES:

RECORD YOUR DREAM

DATE: TIME:

INTERPRETATION

Was this dream from God? ☐ Yes ☐ No

(If the dream was not from God, it does not require an interpretation. However, still sit with the Lord to identify the source and to see what He would have you do.)

RECORD KEY SYMBOLS

COLOURS / SHADES / SHAPES / NUMBERS
NAMES / PEOPLE / BODY PARTS / CHARACTERISTICS
PLACES / TIMES / DATES / POSITIONS
THOUGHTS / FEELINGS / SOUNDS / SMELLS
OBJECTS / ACTIONS / ANIMALS / VEHICLES / FOOD

RECORD UNDERSTANDING

WHAT GOD IS SAYING...
KEY SCRIPTURES:

RECORD YOUR DREAM

DATE: TIME:

INTERPRETATION

Was this dream from God? ☐ Yes ☐ No

(If the dream was not from God, it does not require an interpretation. However, still sit with the Lord to identify the source and to see what He would have you do.)

RECORD KEY SYMBOLS

COLOURS / SHADES / SHAPES / NUMBERS
NAMES / PEOPLE / BODY PARTS / CHARACTERISTICS
PLACES / TIMES / DATES / POSITIONS
THOUGHTS / FEELINGS / SOUNDS / SMELLS
OBJECTS / ACTIONS / ANIMALS / VEHICLES / FOOD

RECORD UNDERSTANDING

WHAT GOD IS SAYING...
KEY SCRIPTURES:

RECORD YOUR DREAM

DATE: TIME:

INTERPRETATION

Was this dream from God? ☐ Yes ☐ No

(If the dream was not from God, it does not require an interpretation. However, still sit with the Lord to identify the source and to see what He would have you do.)

RECORD KEY SYMBOLS

COLOURS / SHADES / SHAPES / NUMBERS
NAMES / PEOPLE / BODY PARTS / CHARACTERISTICS
PLACES / TIMES / DATES / POSITIONS
THOUGHTS / FEELINGS / SOUNDS / SMELLS
OBJECTS / ACTIONS / ANIMALS / VEHICLES / FOOD

RECORD UNDERSTANDING

WHAT GOD IS SAYING…
KEY SCRIPTURES:

RECORD YOUR DREAM

DATE: TIME:

INTERPRETATION

Was this dream from God? ☐ Yes ☐ No

(If the dream was not from God, it does not require an interpretation. However, still sit with the Lord to identify the source and to see what He would have you do.)

RECORD KEY SYMBOLS

COLOURS / SHADES / SHAPES / NUMBERS
NAMES / PEOPLE / BODY PARTS / CHARACTERISTICS
PLACES / TIMES / DATES / POSITIONS
THOUGHTS / FEELINGS / SOUNDS / SMELLS
OBJECTS / ACTIONS / ANIMALS / VEHICLES / FOOD

RECORD UNDERSTANDING

WHAT GOD IS SAYING...
KEY SCRIPTURES:

RECORD YOUR DREAM

DATE: TIME:

INTERPRETATION

Was this dream from God? ☐ Yes ☐ No

(If the dream was not from God, it does not require an interpretation. However, still sit with the Lord to identify the source and to see what He would have you do.)

RECORD KEY SYMBOLS

COLOURS / SHADES / SHAPES / NUMBERS
NAMES / PEOPLE / BODY PARTS / CHARACTERISTICS
PLACES / TIMES / DATES / POSITIONS
THOUGHTS / FEELINGS / SOUNDS / SMELLS
OBJECTS / ACTIONS / ANIMALS / VEHICLES / FOOD

RECORD UNDERSTANDING

WHAT GOD IS SAYING...
KEY SCRIPTURES:

NOTES.

And it shall come to pass in the last days, saith God,
I will pour out of My Spirit upon all flesh: and your sons
and your daughters shall prophesy,
and your young men shall see visions,
and your old men shall
dream dreams:
(ACTS 2:17)

RECORD YOUR DREAM

DATE: TIME:

INTERPRETATION

Was this dream from God? ☐ Yes ☐ No

(If the dream was not from God, it does not require an interpretation. However, still sit with the Lord to identify the source and to see what He would have you do.)

RECORD KEY SYMBOLS

COLOURS / SHADES / SHAPES / NUMBERS
NAMES / PEOPLE / BODY PARTS / CHARACTERISTICS
PLACES / TIMES / DATES / POSITIONS
THOUGHTS / FEELINGS / SOUNDS / SMELLS
OBJECTS / ACTIONS / ANIMALS / VEHICLES / FOOD

RECORD UNDERSTANDING

WHAT GOD IS SAYING...
KEY SCRIPTURES:

RECORD YOUR DREAM

DATE: TIME:

INTERPRETATION

Was this dream from God? ☐ Yes ☐ No

(If the dream was not from God, it does not require an interpretation. However, still sit with the Lord to identify the source and to see what He would have you do.)

RECORD KEY SYMBOLS

COLOURS / SHADES / SHAPES / NUMBERS
NAMES / PEOPLE / BODY PARTS / CHARACTERISTICS
PLACES / TIMES / DATES / POSITIONS
THOUGHTS / FEELINGS / SOUNDS / SMELLS
OBJECTS / ACTIONS / ANIMALS / VEHICLES / FOOD

RECORD UNDERSTANDING

WHAT GOD IS SAYING…
KEY SCRIPTURES:

RECORD YOUR DREAM

DATE: TIME:

INTERPRETATION

Was this dream from God? ☐ Yes ☐ No

(If the dream was not from God, it does not require an interpretation. However, still sit with the Lord to identify the source and to see what He would have you do.)

RECORD KEY SYMBOLS

COLOURS / SHADES / SHAPES / NUMBERS
NAMES / PEOPLE / BODY PARTS / CHARACTERISTICS
PLACES / TIMES / DATES / POSITIONS
THOUGHTS / FEELINGS / SOUNDS / SMELLS
OBJECTS / ACTIONS / ANIMALS / VEHICLES / FOOD

RECORD UNDERSTANDING

WHAT GOD IS SAYING...
KEY SCRIPTURES:

RECORD YOUR DREAM

DATE: TIME:

INTERPRETATION

Was this dream from God? ☐ Yes ☐ No

(If the dream was not from God, it does not require an interpretation. However, still sit with the Lord to identify the source and to see what He would have you do.)

RECORD KEY SYMBOLS

COLOURS / SHADES / SHAPES / NUMBERS
NAMES / PEOPLE / BODY PARTS / CHARACTERISTICS
PLACES / TIMES / DATES / POSITIONS
THOUGHTS / FEELINGS / SOUNDS / SMELLS
OBJECTS / ACTIONS / ANIMALS / VEHICLES / FOOD

RECORD UNDERSTANDING

WHAT GOD IS SAYING...
KEY SCRIPTURES:

RECORD YOUR DREAM

DATE: TIME:

INTERPRETATION

Was this dream from God? ☐ Yes ☐ No

(If the dream was not from God, it does not require an interpretation. However, still sit with the Lord to identify the source and to see what He would have you do.)

RECORD KEY SYMBOLS

COLOURS / SHADES / SHAPES / NUMBERS
NAMES / PEOPLE / BODY PARTS / CHARACTERISTICS
PLACES / TIMES / DATES / POSITIONS
THOUGHTS / FEELINGS / SOUNDS / SMELLS
OBJECTS / ACTIONS / ANIMALS / VEHICLES / FOOD

RECORD UNDERSTANDING

WHAT GOD IS SAYING...
KEY SCRIPTURES:

RECORD YOUR DREAM

DATE: TIME:

INTERPRETATION

Was this dream from God? ☐ Yes ☐ No

(If the dream was not from God, it does not require an interpretation. However, still sit with the Lord to identify the source and to see what He would have you do.)

RECORD KEY SYMBOLS

COLOURS / SHADES / SHAPES / NUMBERS
NAMES / PEOPLE / BODY PARTS / CHARACTERISTICS
PLACES / TIMES / DATES / POSITIONS
THOUGHTS / FEELINGS / SOUNDS / SMELLS
OBJECTS / ACTIONS / ANIMALS / VEHICLES / FOOD

RECORD UNDERSTANDING

WHAT GOD IS SAYING...
KEY SCRIPTURES:

NOTES.

As for these four children, God gave them knowledge and skill in all learning and wisdom: and Daniel had **understanding** in all visions and **dreams**.
(DANIEL 1:17)

RECORD YOUR DREAM

DATE: TIME:

INTERPRETATION

Was this dream from God? ☐ Yes ☐ No

(If the dream was not from God, it does not require an interpretation. However, still sit with the Lord to identify the source and to see what He would have you do.)

RECORD KEY SYMBOLS

COLOURS / SHADES / SHAPES / NUMBERS
NAMES / PEOPLE / BODY PARTS / CHARACTERISTICS
PLACES / TIMES / DATES / POSITIONS
THOUGHTS / FEELINGS / SOUNDS / SMELLS
OBJECTS / ACTIONS / ANIMALS / VEHICLES / FOOD

RECORD UNDERSTANDING

WHAT GOD IS SAYING...
KEY SCRIPTURES:

RECORD YOUR DREAM

DATE: TIME:

INTERPRETATION

Was this dream from God? ☐ Yes ☐ No

(If the dream was not from God, it does not require an interpretation. However, still sit with the Lord to identify the source and to see what He would have you do.)

RECORD KEY SYMBOLS

COLOURS / SHADES / SHAPES / NUMBERS
NAMES / PEOPLE / BODY PARTS / CHARACTERISTICS
PLACES / TIMES / DATES / POSITIONS
THOUGHTS / FEELINGS / SOUNDS / SMELLS
OBJECTS / ACTIONS / ANIMALS / VEHICLES / FOOD

RECORD UNDERSTANDING

WHAT GOD IS SAYING...
KEY SCRIPTURES:

RECORD YOUR DREAM

DATE: TIME:

INTERPRETATION

Was this dream from God? ☐ Yes ☐ No

(If the dream was not from God, it does not require an interpretation. However, still sit with the Lord to identify the source and to see what He would have you do.)

RECORD KEY SYMBOLS

COLOURS / SHADES / SHAPES / NUMBERS
NAMES / PEOPLE / BODY PARTS / CHARACTERISTICS
PLACES / TIMES / DATES / POSITIONS
THOUGHTS / FEELINGS / SOUNDS / SMELLS
OBJECTS / ACTIONS / ANIMALS / VEHICLES / FOOD

RECORD UNDERSTANDING

WHAT GOD IS SAYING…
KEY SCRIPTURES:

RECORD YOUR DREAM

DATE: TIME:

INTERPRETATION

Was this dream from God? ☐ Yes ☐ No

(If the dream was not from God, it does not require an interpretation. However, still sit with the Lord to identify the source and to see what He would have you do.)

RECORD KEY SYMBOLS

COLOURS / SHADES / SHAPES / NUMBERS
NAMES / PEOPLE / BODY PARTS / CHARACTERISTICS
PLACES / TIMES / DATES / POSITIONS
THOUGHTS / FEELINGS / SOUNDS / SMELLS
OBJECTS / ACTIONS / ANIMALS / VEHICLES / FOOD

RECORD UNDERSTANDING

WHAT GOD IS SAYING...
KEY SCRIPTURES:

RECORD YOUR DREAM

DATE: TIME:

INTERPRETATION

Was this dream from God? ☐ Yes ☐ No

(If the dream was not from God, it does not require an interpretation. However, still sit with the Lord to identify the source and to see what He would have you do.)

RECORD KEY SYMBOLS

COLOURS / SHADES / SHAPES / NUMBERS
NAMES / PEOPLE / BODY PARTS / CHARACTERISTICS
PLACES / TIMES / DATES / POSITIONS
THOUGHTS / FEELINGS / SOUNDS / SMELLS
OBJECTS / ACTIONS / ANIMALS / VEHICLES / FOOD

RECORD UNDERSTANDING

WHAT GOD IS SAYING...
KEY SCRIPTURES:

RECORD YOUR DREAM

DATE: TIME:

INTERPRETATION

Was this dream from God? ☐ Yes ☐ No

(If the dream was not from God, it does not require an interpretation. However, still sit with the Lord to identify the source and to see what He would have you do.)

RECORD KEY SYMBOLS

COLOURS / SHADES / SHAPES / NUMBERS
NAMES / PEOPLE / BODY PARTS / CHARACTERISTICS
PLACES / TIMES / DATES / POSITIONS
THOUGHTS / FEELINGS / SOUNDS / SMELLS
OBJECTS / ACTIONS / ANIMALS / VEHICLES / FOOD

RECORD UNDERSTANDING

WHAT GOD IS SAYING…
KEY SCRIPTURES:

NOTES.

And they said unto him, We have dreamed a **dream**,
and there is no interpreter of it. And Joseph said unto
them, Do not **interpretations** belong to God?
tell me them, I pray you.
(GENESIS 40:8)

RECORD YOUR DREAM

DATE: TIME:

INTERPRETATION

Was this dream from God? ☐ Yes ☐ No

(If the dream was not from God, it does not require an interpretation. However, still sit with the Lord to identify the source and to see what He would have you do.)

RECORD KEY SYMBOLS

COLOURS / SHADES / SHAPES / NUMBERS
NAMES / PEOPLE / BODY PARTS / CHARACTERISTICS
PLACES / TIMES / DATES / POSITIONS
THOUGHTS / FEELINGS / SOUNDS / SMELLS
OBJECTS / ACTIONS / ANIMALS / VEHICLES / FOOD

RECORD UNDERSTANDING

WHAT GOD IS SAYING...
KEY SCRIPTURES:

RECORD YOUR DREAM

DATE: TIME:

INTERPRETATION

Was this dream from God? ☐ Yes ☐ No

(If the dream was not from God, it does not require an interpretation. However, still sit with the Lord to identify the source and to see what He would have you do.)

RECORD KEY SYMBOLS

COLOURS / SHADES / SHAPES / NUMBERS
NAMES / PEOPLE / BODY PARTS / CHARACTERISTICS
PLACES / TIMES / DATES / POSITIONS
THOUGHTS / FEELINGS / SOUNDS / SMELLS
OBJECTS / ACTIONS / ANIMALS / VEHICLES / FOOD

RECORD UNDERSTANDING

WHAT GOD IS SAYING...
KEY SCRIPTURES:

RECORD YOUR DREAM

DATE: TIME:

INTERPRETATION

Was this dream from God? ☐ Yes ☐ No

(If the dream was not from God, it does not require an interpretation. However, still sit with the Lord to identify the source and to see what He would have you do.)

RECORD KEY SYMBOLS

COLOURS / SHADES / SHAPES / NUMBERS
NAMES / PEOPLE / BODY PARTS / CHARACTERISTICS
PLACES / TIMES / DATES / POSITIONS
THOUGHTS / FEELINGS / SOUNDS / SMELLS
OBJECTS / ACTIONS / ANIMALS / VEHICLES / FOOD

RECORD UNDERSTANDING

WHAT GOD IS SAYING...
KEY SCRIPTURES:

RECORD YOUR DREAM

DATE: TIME:

INTERPRETATION

Was this dream from God? ☐ Yes ☐ No

(If the dream was not from God, it does not require an interpretation. However, still sit with the Lord to identify the source and to see what He would have you do.)

RECORD KEY SYMBOLS

COLOURS / SHADES / SHAPES / NUMBERS
NAMES / PEOPLE / BODY PARTS / CHARACTERISTICS
PLACES / TIMES / DATES / POSITIONS
THOUGHTS / FEELINGS / SOUNDS / SMELLS
OBJECTS / ACTIONS / ANIMALS / VEHICLES / FOOD

RECORD UNDERSTANDING

WHAT GOD IS SAYING...
KEY SCRIPTURES:

RECORD YOUR DREAM

DATE: TIME:

INTERPRETATION

Was this dream from God? ☐ Yes ☐ No

(If the dream was not from God, it does not require an interpretation. However, still sit with the Lord to identify the source and to see what He would have you do.)

RECORD KEY SYMBOLS

COLOURS / SHADES / SHAPES / NUMBERS
NAMES / PEOPLE / BODY PARTS / CHARACTERISTICS
PLACES / TIMES / DATES / POSITIONS
THOUGHTS / FEELINGS / SOUNDS / SMELLS
OBJECTS / ACTIONS / ANIMALS / VEHICLES / FOOD

RECORD UNDERSTANDING

WHAT GOD IS SAYING...
KEY SCRIPTURES:

RECORD YOUR DREAM

DATE: TIME:

INTERPRETATION

Was this dream from God? ☐ Yes ☐ No

(If the dream was not from God, it does not require an interpretation. However, still sit with the Lord to identify the source and to see what He would have you do.)

RECORD KEY SYMBOLS

COLOURS / SHADES / SHAPES / NUMBERS
NAMES / PEOPLE / BODY PARTS / CHARACTERISTICS
PLACES / TIMES / DATES / POSITIONS
THOUGHTS / FEELINGS / SOUNDS / SMELLS
OBJECTS / ACTIONS / ANIMALS / VEHICLES / FOOD

RECORD UNDERSTANDING

WHAT GOD IS SAYING...
KEY SCRIPTURES:

NOTES.

And when they were departed, behold, the angel of the Lord appeareth to Joseph in a **dream**, saying, Arise, and take the young child and His mother, and flee into Egypt, and be thou there until I bring thee word: for Herod will seek the young child to destroy Him.
(MATTHEW 2:13)

RECORD YOUR DREAM

DATE: TIME:

INTERPRETATION

Was this dream from God? ☐ Yes ☐ No

(If the dream was not from God, it does not require an interpretation. However, still sit with the Lord to identify the source and to see what He would have you do.)

RECORD KEY SYMBOLS

COLOURS / SHADES / SHAPES / NUMBERS
NAMES / PEOPLE / BODY PARTS / CHARACTERISTICS
PLACES / TIMES / DATES / POSITIONS
THOUGHTS / FEELINGS / SOUNDS / SMELLS
OBJECTS / ACTIONS / ANIMALS / VEHICLES / FOOD

RECORD UNDERSTANDING

WHAT GOD IS SAYING...
KEY SCRIPTURES:

RECORD YOUR DREAM

DATE: TIME:

INTERPRETATION

Was this dream from God? ☐ Yes ☐ No

(If the dream was not from God, it does not require an interpretation. However, still sit with the Lord to identify the source and to see what He would have you do.)

RECORD KEY SYMBOLS

COLOURS / SHADES / SHAPES / NUMBERS
NAMES / PEOPLE / BODY PARTS / CHARACTERISTICS
PLACES / TIMES / DATES / POSITIONS
THOUGHTS / FEELINGS / SOUNDS / SMELLS
OBJECTS / ACTIONS / ANIMALS / VEHICLES / FOOD

RECORD UNDERSTANDING

WHAT GOD IS SAYING...
KEY SCRIPTURES:

RECORD YOUR DREAM

DATE: TIME:

INTERPRETATION

Was this dream from God? ☐ Yes ☐ No

(If the dream was not from God, it does not require an interpretation. However, still sit with the Lord to identify the source and to see what He would have you do.)

RECORD KEY SYMBOLS

COLOURS / SHADES / SHAPES / NUMBERS
NAMES / PEOPLE / BODY PARTS / CHARACTERISTICS
PLACES / TIMES / DATES / POSITIONS
THOUGHTS / FEELINGS / SOUNDS / SMELLS
OBJECTS / ACTIONS / ANIMALS / VEHICLES / FOOD

RECORD UNDERSTANDING

WHAT GOD IS SAYING...
KEY SCRIPTURES:

RECORD YOUR DREAM

DATE: TIME:

INTERPRETATION

Was this dream from God? ☐ Yes ☐ No

(If the dream was not from God, it does not require an interpretation. However, still sit with the Lord to identify the source and to see what He would have you do.)

RECORD KEY SYMBOLS

COLOURS / SHADES / SHAPES / NUMBERS
NAMES / PEOPLE / BODY PARTS / CHARACTERISTICS
PLACES / TIMES / DATES / POSITIONS
THOUGHTS / FEELINGS / SOUNDS / SMELLS
OBJECTS / ACTIONS / ANIMALS / VEHICLES / FOOD

RECORD UNDERSTANDING

WHAT GOD IS SAYING...
KEY SCRIPTURES:

RECORD YOUR DREAM

DATE: TIME:

INTERPRETATION

Was this dream from God? ☐ Yes ☐ No

(If the dream was not from God, it does not require an interpretation. However, still sit with the Lord to identify the source and to see what He would have you do.)

RECORD KEY SYMBOLS

COLOURS / SHADES / SHAPES / NUMBERS
NAMES / PEOPLE / BODY PARTS / CHARACTERISTICS
PLACES / TIMES / DATES / POSITIONS
THOUGHTS / FEELINGS / SOUNDS / SMELLS
OBJECTS / ACTIONS / ANIMALS / VEHICLES / FOOD

RECORD UNDERSTANDING

WHAT GOD IS SAYING...
KEY SCRIPTURES:

RECORD YOUR DREAM

DATE: TIME:

INTERPRETATION

Was this dream from God? ☐ Yes ☐ No

(If the dream was not from God, it does not require an interpretation. However, still sit with the Lord to identify the source and to see what He would have you do.)

RECORD KEY SYMBOLS

COLOURS / SHADES / SHAPES / NUMBERS
NAMES / PEOPLE / BODY PARTS / CHARACTERISTICS
PLACES / TIMES / DATES / POSITIONS
THOUGHTS / FEELINGS / SOUNDS / SMELLS
OBJECTS / ACTIONS / ANIMALS / VEHICLES / FOOD

RECORD UNDERSTANDING

WHAT GOD IS SAYING...
KEY SCRIPTURES:

NOTES.

In the first year of Belshazzar king of Babylon Daniel had a **dream** and visions of his head upon his bed: then he **wrote the dream**, and told the sum of the matters. (DANIEL 7:1)

RECORD YOUR DREAM

DATE: TIME:

INTERPRETATION

Was this dream from God? ☐ Yes ☐ No

(If the dream was not from God, it does not require an interpretation. However, still sit with the Lord to identify the source and to see what He would have you do.)

RECORD KEY SYMBOLS

COLOURS / SHADES / SHAPES / NUMBERS
NAMES / PEOPLE / BODY PARTS / CHARACTERISTICS
PLACES / TIMES / DATES / POSITIONS
THOUGHTS / FEELINGS / SOUNDS / SMELLS
OBJECTS / ACTIONS / ANIMALS / VEHICLES / FOOD

RECORD UNDERSTANDING

WHAT GOD IS SAYING...
KEY SCRIPTURES:

RECORD YOUR DREAM

DATE: TIME:

INTERPRETATION

Was this dream from God? ☐ Yes ☐ No

(If the dream was not from God, it does not require an interpretation. However, still sit with the Lord to identify the source and to see what He would have you do.)

RECORD KEY SYMBOLS

COLOURS / SHADES / SHAPES / NUMBERS
NAMES / PEOPLE / BODY PARTS / CHARACTERISTICS
PLACES / TIMES / DATES / POSITIONS
THOUGHTS / FEELINGS / SOUNDS / SMELLS
OBJECTS / ACTIONS / ANIMALS / VEHICLES / FOOD

RECORD UNDERSTANDING

WHAT GOD IS SAYING…
KEY SCRIPTURES:

RECORD YOUR DREAM

DATE: TIME:

INTERPRETATION

Was this dream from God? ☐ Yes ☐ No

(If the dream was not from God, it does not require an interpretation. However, still sit with the Lord to identify the source and to see what He would have you do.)

RECORD KEY SYMBOLS

COLOURS / SHADES / SHAPES / NUMBERS
NAMES / PEOPLE / BODY PARTS / CHARACTERISTICS
PLACES / TIMES / DATES / POSITIONS
THOUGHTS / FEELINGS / SOUNDS / SMELLS
OBJECTS / ACTIONS / ANIMALS / VEHICLES / FOOD

RECORD UNDERSTANDING

WHAT GOD IS SAYING…
KEY SCRIPTURES:

RECORD YOUR DREAM

DATE: TIME:

INTERPRETATION

Was this dream from God? ☐ Yes ☐ No

(If the dream was not from God, it does not require an interpretation. However, still sit with the Lord to identify the source and to see what He would have you do.)

RECORD KEY SYMBOLS

COLOURS / SHADES / SHAPES / NUMBERS
NAMES / PEOPLE / BODY PARTS / CHARACTERISTICS
PLACES / TIMES / DATES / POSITIONS
THOUGHTS / FEELINGS / SOUNDS / SMELLS
OBJECTS / ACTIONS / ANIMALS / VEHICLES / FOOD

RECORD UNDERSTANDING

WHAT GOD IS SAYING...
KEY SCRIPTURES:

RECORD YOUR DREAM

DATE: TIME:

INTERPRETATION

Was this dream from God? ☐ Yes ☐ No

(If the dream was not from God, it does not require an interpretation. However, still sit with the Lord to identify the source and to see what He would have you do.)

RECORD KEY SYMBOLS

COLOURS / SHADES / SHAPES / NUMBERS
NAMES / PEOPLE / BODY PARTS / CHARACTERISTICS
PLACES / TIMES / DATES / POSITIONS
THOUGHTS / FEELINGS / SOUNDS / SMELLS
OBJECTS / ACTIONS / ANIMALS / VEHICLES / FOOD

RECORD UNDERSTANDING

WHAT GOD IS SAYING…
KEY SCRIPTURES:

RECORD YOUR DREAM

DATE: TIME:

INTERPRETATION

Was this dream from God? ☐ Yes ☐ No

(If the dream was not from God, it does not require an interpretation. However, still sit with the Lord to identify the source and to see what He would have you do.)

RECORD KEY SYMBOLS

COLOURS / SHADES / SHAPES / NUMBERS
NAMES / PEOPLE / BODY PARTS / CHARACTERISTICS
PLACES / TIMES / DATES / POSITIONS
THOUGHTS / FEELINGS / SOUNDS / SMELLS
OBJECTS / ACTIONS / ANIMALS / VEHICLES / FOOD

RECORD UNDERSTANDING

WHAT GOD IS SAYING...
KEY SCRIPTURES:

NOTES.

And Joseph said unto Pharaoh,
The **dream** of Pharaoh is one:
God hath shewed Pharaoh **what He is about to do.**
(GENESIS 41:25)

RECORD YOUR DREAM

DATE: TIME:

INTERPRETATION

Was this dream from God? ☐ Yes ☐ No

(If the dream was not from God, it does not require an interpretation. However, still sit with the Lord to identify the source and to see what He would have you do.)

RECORD KEY SYMBOLS

COLOURS / SHADES / SHAPES / NUMBERS
NAMES / PEOPLE / BODY PARTS / CHARACTERISTICS
PLACES / TIMES / DATES / POSITIONS
THOUGHTS / FEELINGS / SOUNDS / SMELLS
OBJECTS / ACTIONS / ANIMALS / VEHICLES / FOOD

RECORD UNDERSTANDING

WHAT GOD IS SAYING…
KEY SCRIPTURES:

RECORD YOUR DREAM

DATE: TIME:

INTERPRETATION

Was this dream from God? ☐ Yes ☐ No

(If the dream was not from God, it does not require an interpretation. However, still sit with the Lord to identify the source and to see what He would have you do.)

RECORD KEY SYMBOLS

COLOURS / SHADES / SHAPES / NUMBERS
NAMES / PEOPLE / BODY PARTS / CHARACTERISTICS
PLACES / TIMES / DATES / POSITIONS
THOUGHTS / FEELINGS / SOUNDS / SMELLS
OBJECTS / ACTIONS / ANIMALS / VEHICLES / FOOD

RECORD UNDERSTANDING

WHAT GOD IS SAYING...
KEY SCRIPTURES:

RECORD YOUR DREAM

DATE:

TIME:

INTERPRETATION

Was this dream from God? ☐ Yes ☐ No

(If the dream was not from God, it does not require an interpretation. However, still sit with the Lord to identify the source and to see what He would have you do.)

RECORD KEY SYMBOLS

COLOURS / SHADES / SHAPES / NUMBERS
NAMES / PEOPLE / BODY PARTS / CHARACTERISTICS
PLACES / TIMES / DATES / POSITIONS
THOUGHTS / FEELINGS / SOUNDS / SMELLS
OBJECTS / ACTIONS / ANIMALS / VEHICLES / FOOD

RECORD UNDERSTANDING

WHAT GOD IS SAYING...
KEY SCRIPTURES:

RECORD YOUR DREAM

DATE: TIME:

INTERPRETATION

Was this dream from God? ☐ Yes ☐ No

(If the dream was not from God, it does not require an interpretation. However, still sit with the Lord to identify the source and to see what He would have you do.)

RECORD KEY SYMBOLS

COLOURS / SHADES / SHAPES / NUMBERS
NAMES / PEOPLE / BODY PARTS / CHARACTERISTICS
PLACES / TIMES / DATES / POSITIONS
THOUGHTS / FEELINGS / SOUNDS / SMELLS
OBJECTS / ACTIONS / ANIMALS / VEHICLES / FOOD

RECORD UNDERSTANDING

WHAT GOD IS SAYING...
KEY SCRIPTURES:

RECORD YOUR DREAM

DATE: TIME:

INTERPRETATION

Was this dream from God? ☐ Yes ☐ No

(If the dream was not from God, it does not require an interpretation. However, still sit with the Lord to identify the source and to see what He would have you do.)

RECORD KEY SYMBOLS

COLOURS / SHADES / SHAPES / NUMBERS
NAMES / PEOPLE / BODY PARTS / CHARACTERISTICS
PLACES / TIMES / DATES / POSITIONS
THOUGHTS / FEELINGS / SOUNDS / SMELLS
OBJECTS / ACTIONS / ANIMALS / VEHICLES / FOOD

RECORD UNDERSTANDING

WHAT GOD IS SAYING...
KEY SCRIPTURES:

RECORD YOUR DREAM

DATE: TIME:

INTERPRETATION

Was this dream from God? ☐ Yes ☐ No

(If the dream was not from God, it does not require an interpretation. However, still sit with the Lord to identify the source and to see what He would have you do.)

RECORD KEY SYMBOLS

COLOURS / SHADES / SHAPES / NUMBERS
NAMES / PEOPLE / BODY PARTS / CHARACTERISTICS
PLACES / TIMES / DATES / POSITIONS
THOUGHTS / FEELINGS / SOUNDS / SMELLS
OBJECTS / ACTIONS / ANIMALS / VEHICLES / FOOD

RECORD UNDERSTANDING

WHAT GOD IS SAYING...
KEY SCRIPTURES:

NOTES.

For **God speaketh** once, yea twice,
yet man perceiveth it not.
In a dream, in a vision of the night, when deep sleep
falleth upon men, in slumberings upon the bed;
(JOB 33:14-15)

RECORD YOUR DREAM

DATE: TIME:

INTERPRETATION

Was this dream from God? ☐ Yes ☐ No

(If the dream was not from God, it does not require an interpretation. However, still sit with the Lord to identify the source and to see what He would have you do.)

RECORD KEY SYMBOLS

COLOURS / SHADES / SHAPES / NUMBERS
NAMES / PEOPLE / BODY PARTS / CHARACTERISTICS
PLACES / TIMES / DATES / POSITIONS
THOUGHTS / FEELINGS / SOUNDS / SMELLS
OBJECTS / ACTIONS / ANIMALS / VEHICLES / FOOD

RECORD UNDERSTANDING

WHAT GOD IS SAYING...
KEY SCRIPTURES:

RECORD YOUR DREAM

DATE: TIME:

INTERPRETATION

Was this dream from God? ☐ Yes ☐ No

(If the dream was not from God, it does not require an interpretation. However, still sit with the Lord to identify the source and to see what He would have you do.)

RECORD KEY SYMBOLS

COLOURS / SHADES / SHAPES / NUMBERS
NAMES / PEOPLE / BODY PARTS / CHARACTERISTICS
PLACES / TIMES / DATES / POSITIONS
THOUGHTS / FEELINGS / SOUNDS / SMELLS
OBJECTS / ACTIONS / ANIMALS / VEHICLES / FOOD

RECORD UNDERSTANDING

WHAT GOD IS SAYING...
KEY SCRIPTURES:

RECORD YOUR DREAM

DATE: TIME:

INTERPRETATION

Was this dream from God? ☐ Yes ☐ No

(If the dream was not from God, it does not require an interpretation. However, still sit with the Lord to identify the source and to see what He would have you do.)

RECORD KEY SYMBOLS

COLOURS / SHADES / SHAPES / NUMBERS
NAMES / PEOPLE / BODY PARTS / CHARACTERISTICS
PLACES / TIMES / DATES / POSITIONS
THOUGHTS / FEELINGS / SOUNDS / SMELLS
OBJECTS / ACTIONS / ANIMALS / VEHICLES / FOOD

RECORD UNDERSTANDING

WHAT GOD IS SAYING...
KEY SCRIPTURES:

RECORD YOUR DREAM

DATE: TIME:

INTERPRETATION

Was this dream from God? ☐ Yes ☐ No

(If the dream was not from God, it does not require an interpretation. However, still sit with the Lord to identify the source and to see what He would have you do.)

RECORD KEY SYMBOLS

COLOURS / SHADES / SHAPES / NUMBERS
NAMES / PEOPLE / BODY PARTS / CHARACTERISTICS
PLACES / TIMES / DATES / POSITIONS
THOUGHTS / FEELINGS / SOUNDS / SMELLS
OBJECTS / ACTIONS / ANIMALS / VEHICLES / FOOD

RECORD UNDERSTANDING

WHAT GOD IS SAYING...
KEY SCRIPTURES:

RECORD YOUR DREAM

DATE: TIME:

INTERPRETATION

Was this dream from God? ☐ Yes ☐ No

(If the dream was not from God, it does not require an interpretation. However, still sit with the Lord to identify the source and to see what He would have you do.)

RECORD KEY SYMBOLS

COLOURS / SHADES / SHAPES / NUMBERS
NAMES / PEOPLE / BODY PARTS / CHARACTERISTICS
PLACES / TIMES / DATES / POSITIONS
THOUGHTS / FEELINGS / SOUNDS / SMELLS
OBJECTS / ACTIONS / ANIMALS / VEHICLES / FOOD

RECORD UNDERSTANDING

WHAT GOD IS SAYING...
KEY SCRIPTURES:

RECORD YOUR DREAM

DATE: TIME:

INTERPRETATION

Was this dream from God? ☐ Yes ☐ No

(If the dream was not from God, it does not require an interpretation. However, still sit with the Lord to identify the source and to see what He would have you do.)

RECORD KEY SYMBOLS

COLOURS / SHADES / SHAPES / NUMBERS
NAMES / PEOPLE / BODY PARTS / CHARACTERISTICS
PLACES / TIMES / DATES / POSITIONS
THOUGHTS / FEELINGS / SOUNDS / SMELLS
OBJECTS / ACTIONS / ANIMALS / VEHICLES / FOOD

RECORD UNDERSTANDING

WHAT GOD IS SAYING...
KEY SCRIPTURES:

NOTES.

But **while he thought on these things**, behold,
the angel of the Lord appeared unto him in a **dream**,
saying, Joseph, thou son of David,
fear not to take unto thee Mary thy wife:
for that which is conceived in her is of the Holy Ghost.
(MATTHEW 1:20)

RECORD YOUR DREAM

DATE: TIME:

INTERPRETATION

Was this dream from God? ☐ Yes ☐ No

(If the dream was not from God, it does not require an interpretation. However, still sit with the Lord to identify the source and to see what He would have you do.)

RECORD KEY SYMBOLS

COLOURS / SHADES / SHAPES / NUMBERS
NAMES / PEOPLE / BODY PARTS / CHARACTERISTICS
PLACES / TIMES / DATES / POSITIONS
THOUGHTS / FEELINGS / SOUNDS / SMELLS
OBJECTS / ACTIONS / ANIMALS / VEHICLES / FOOD

RECORD UNDERSTANDING

WHAT GOD IS SAYING...
KEY SCRIPTURES:

RECORD YOUR DREAM

DATE: TIME:

INTERPRETATION

Was this dream from God? ☐ Yes ☐ No

(If the dream was not from God, it does not require an interpretation. However, still sit with the Lord to identify the source and to see what He would have you do.)

RECORD KEY SYMBOLS

COLOURS / SHADES / SHAPES / NUMBERS
NAMES / PEOPLE / BODY PARTS / CHARACTERISTICS
PLACES / TIMES / DATES / POSITIONS
THOUGHTS / FEELINGS / SOUNDS / SMELLS
OBJECTS / ACTIONS / ANIMALS / VEHICLES / FOOD

RECORD UNDERSTANDING

WHAT GOD IS SAYING...
KEY SCRIPTURES:

RECORD YOUR DREAM

DATE: TIME:

INTERPRETATION

Was this dream from God? ☐ Yes ☐ No

(If the dream was not from God, it does not require an interpretation. However, still sit with the Lord to identify the source and to see what He would have you do.)

RECORD KEY SYMBOLS

COLOURS / SHADES / SHAPES / NUMBERS
NAMES / PEOPLE / BODY PARTS / CHARACTERISTICS
PLACES / TIMES / DATES / POSITIONS
THOUGHTS / FEELINGS / SOUNDS / SMELLS
OBJECTS / ACTIONS / ANIMALS / VEHICLES / FOOD

RECORD UNDERSTANDING

WHAT GOD IS SAYING…
KEY SCRIPTURES:

RECORD YOUR DREAM

DATE:

TIME:

INTERPRETATION

Was this dream from God? ☐ Yes ☐ No

(If the dream was not from God, it does not require an interpretation. However, still sit with the Lord to identify the source and to see what He would have you do.)

RECORD KEY SYMBOLS

COLOURS / SHADES / SHAPES / NUMBERS
NAMES / PEOPLE / BODY PARTS / CHARACTERISTICS
PLACES / TIMES / DATES / POSITIONS
THOUGHTS / FEELINGS / SOUNDS / SMELLS
OBJECTS / ACTIONS / ANIMALS / VEHICLES / FOOD

RECORD UNDERSTANDING

WHAT GOD IS SAYING...
KEY SCRIPTURES:

RECORD YOUR DREAM

DATE: TIME:

INTERPRETATION

Was this dream from God? ☐ Yes ☐ No

(If the dream was not from God, it does not require an interpretation. However, still sit with the Lord to identify the source and to see what He would have you do.)

RECORD KEY SYMBOLS

COLOURS / SHADES / SHAPES / NUMBERS
NAMES / PEOPLE / BODY PARTS / CHARACTERISTICS
PLACES / TIMES / DATES / POSITIONS
THOUGHTS / FEELINGS / SOUNDS / SMELLS
OBJECTS / ACTIONS / ANIMALS / VEHICLES / FOOD

RECORD UNDERSTANDING

WHAT GOD IS SAYING...
KEY SCRIPTURES:

RECORD YOUR DREAM

DATE: TIME:

INTERPRETATION

Was this dream from God? ☐ Yes ☐ No

(If the dream was not from God, it does not require an interpretation. However, still sit with the Lord to identify the source and to see what He would have you do.)

RECORD KEY SYMBOLS

COLOURS / SHADES / SHAPES / NUMBERS
NAMES / PEOPLE / BODY PARTS / CHARACTERISTICS
PLACES / TIMES / DATES / POSITIONS
THOUGHTS / FEELINGS / SOUNDS / SMELLS
OBJECTS / ACTIONS / ANIMALS / VEHICLES / FOOD

RECORD UNDERSTANDING

WHAT GOD IS SAYING...
KEY SCRIPTURES:

NOTES.

And **being warned of God in a dream**
that they should not return to Herod,
they departed into their own country another way.
(MATTHEW 2:12)

RECORD YOUR DREAM

DATE: TIME:

INTERPRETATION

Was this dream from God? ☐ Yes ☐ No

(If the dream was not from God, it does not require an interpretation. However, still sit with the Lord to identify the source and to see what He would have you do.)

RECORD KEY SYMBOLS

COLOURS / SHADES / SHAPES / NUMBERS
NAMES / PEOPLE / BODY PARTS / CHARACTERISTICS
PLACES / TIMES / DATES / POSITIONS
THOUGHTS / FEELINGS / SOUNDS / SMELLS
OBJECTS / ACTIONS / ANIMALS / VEHICLES / FOOD

RECORD UNDERSTANDING

WHAT GOD IS SAYING...
KEY SCRIPTURES:

RECORD YOUR DREAM

DATE: TIME:

INTERPRETATION

Was this dream from God? ☐ Yes ☐ No

(If the dream was not from God, it does not require an interpretation. However, still sit with the Lord to identify the source and to see what He would have you do.)

RECORD KEY SYMBOLS

COLOURS / SHADES / SHAPES / NUMBERS
NAMES / PEOPLE / BODY PARTS / CHARACTERISTICS
PLACES / TIMES / DATES / POSITIONS
THOUGHTS / FEELINGS / SOUNDS / SMELLS
OBJECTS / ACTIONS / ANIMALS / VEHICLES / FOOD

RECORD UNDERSTANDING

WHAT GOD IS SAYING...
KEY SCRIPTURES:

RECORD YOUR DREAM

DATE: TIME:

INTERPRETATION

Was this dream from God? ☐ Yes ☐ No

(If the dream was not from God, it does not require an interpretation. However, still sit with the Lord to identify the source and to see what He would have you do.)

RECORD KEY SYMBOLS

COLOURS / SHADES / SHAPES / NUMBERS
NAMES / PEOPLE / BODY PARTS / CHARACTERISTICS
PLACES / TIMES / DATES / POSITIONS
THOUGHTS / FEELINGS / SOUNDS / SMELLS
OBJECTS / ACTIONS / ANIMALS / VEHICLES / FOOD

RECORD UNDERSTANDING

WHAT GOD IS SAYING...
KEY SCRIPTURES:

RECORD YOUR DREAM

DATE: TIME:

INTERPRETATION

Was this dream from God? ☐ Yes ☐ No

(If the dream was not from God, it does not require an interpretation. However, still sit with the Lord to identify the source and to see what He would have you do.)

RECORD KEY SYMBOLS

COLOURS / SHADES / SHAPES / NUMBERS
NAMES / PEOPLE / BODY PARTS / CHARACTERISTICS
PLACES / TIMES / DATES / POSITIONS
THOUGHTS / FEELINGS / SOUNDS / SMELLS
OBJECTS / ACTIONS / ANIMALS / VEHICLES / FOOD

RECORD UNDERSTANDING

WHAT GOD IS SAYING...
KEY SCRIPTURES:

RECORD YOUR DREAM

DATE: TIME:

INTERPRETATION

Was this dream from God? ☐ Yes ☐ No

(If the dream was not from God, it does not require an interpretation. However, still sit with the Lord to identify the source and to see what He would have you do.)

RECORD KEY SYMBOLS

COLOURS / SHADES / SHAPES / NUMBERS
NAMES / PEOPLE / BODY PARTS / CHARACTERISTICS
PLACES / TIMES / DATES / POSITIONS
THOUGHTS / FEELINGS / SOUNDS / SMELLS
OBJECTS / ACTIONS / ANIMALS / VEHICLES / FOOD

RECORD UNDERSTANDING

WHAT GOD IS SAYING...
KEY SCRIPTURES:

RECORD YOUR DREAM

DATE: TIME:

INTERPRETATION

Was this dream from God? ☐ Yes ☐ No

(If the dream was not from God, it does not require an interpretation. However, still sit with the Lord to identify the source and to see what He would have you do.)

RECORD KEY SYMBOLS

COLOURS / SHADES / SHAPES / NUMBERS
NAMES / PEOPLE / BODY PARTS / CHARACTERISTICS
PLACES / TIMES / DATES / POSITIONS
THOUGHTS / FEELINGS / SOUNDS / SMELLS
OBJECTS / ACTIONS / ANIMALS / VEHICLES / FOOD

RECORD UNDERSTANDING

WHAT GOD IS SAYING...
KEY SCRIPTURES:

NOTES.

The prophet that hath a **dream**, let him tell a **dream**; and he that hath My word, let him speak My word faithfully. What is the chaff to the wheat? saith the Lord.
(JEREMIAH 23:28)

RECORD YOUR DREAM

DATE: TIME:

INTERPRETATION

Was this dream from God? ☐ Yes ☐ No

(If the dream was not from God, it does not require an interpretation. However, still sit with the Lord to identify the source and to see what He would have you do.)

RECORD KEY SYMBOLS

COLOURS / SHADES / SHAPES / NUMBERS
NAMES / PEOPLE / BODY PARTS / CHARACTERISTICS
PLACES / TIMES / DATES / POSITIONS
THOUGHTS / FEELINGS / SOUNDS / SMELLS
OBJECTS / ACTIONS / ANIMALS / VEHICLES / FOOD

RECORD UNDERSTANDING

WHAT GOD IS SAYING...
KEY SCRIPTURES:

RECORD YOUR DREAM

DATE: TIME:

INTERPRETATION

Was this dream from God? ☐ Yes ☐ No

(If the dream was not from God, it does not require an interpretation. However, still sit with the Lord to identify the source and to see what He would have you do.)

RECORD KEY SYMBOLS

COLOURS / SHADES / SHAPES / NUMBERS
NAMES / PEOPLE / BODY PARTS / CHARACTERISTICS
PLACES / TIMES / DATES / POSITIONS
THOUGHTS / FEELINGS / SOUNDS / SMELLS
OBJECTS / ACTIONS / ANIMALS / VEHICLES / FOOD

RECORD UNDERSTANDING

WHAT GOD IS SAYING...
KEY SCRIPTURES:

RECORD YOUR DREAM

DATE: TIME:

INTERPRETATION

Was this dream from God? ☐ Yes ☐ No

(If the dream was not from God, it does not require an interpretation. However, still sit with the Lord to identify the source and to see what He would have you do.)

RECORD KEY SYMBOLS

COLOURS / SHADES / SHAPES / NUMBERS
NAMES / PEOPLE / BODY PARTS / CHARACTERISTICS
PLACES / TIMES / DATES / POSITIONS
THOUGHTS / FEELINGS / SOUNDS / SMELLS
OBJECTS / ACTIONS / ANIMALS / VEHICLES / FOOD

RECORD UNDERSTANDING

WHAT GOD IS SAYING...
KEY SCRIPTURES:

RECORD YOUR DREAM

DATE: TIME:

INTERPRETATION

Was this dream from God? ☐ Yes ☐ No

(If the dream was not from God, it does not require an interpretation. However, still sit with the Lord to identify the source and to see what He would have you do.)

RECORD KEY SYMBOLS

COLOURS / SHADES / SHAPES / NUMBERS
NAMES / PEOPLE / BODY PARTS / CHARACTERISTICS
PLACES / TIMES / DATES / POSITIONS
THOUGHTS / FEELINGS / SOUNDS / SMELLS
OBJECTS / ACTIONS / ANIMALS / VEHICLES / FOOD

RECORD UNDERSTANDING

WHAT GOD IS SAYING...
KEY SCRIPTURES:

RECORD YOUR DREAM

DATE: TIME:

INTERPRETATION

Was this dream from God? ☐ Yes ☐ No

(If the dream was not from God, it does not require an interpretation. However, still sit with the Lord to identify the source and to see what He would have you do.)

RECORD KEY SYMBOLS

COLOURS / SHADES / SHAPES / NUMBERS
NAMES / PEOPLE / BODY PARTS / CHARACTERISTICS
PLACES / TIMES / DATES / POSITIONS
THOUGHTS / FEELINGS / SOUNDS / SMELLS
OBJECTS / ACTIONS / ANIMALS / VEHICLES / FOOD

RECORD UNDERSTANDING

WHAT GOD IS SAYING...
KEY SCRIPTURES:

RECORD YOUR DREAM

DATE: TIME:

INTERPRETATION

Was this dream from God? ☐ Yes ☐ No

(If the dream was not from God, it does not require an interpretation. However, still sit with the Lord to identify the source and to see what He would have you do.)

RECORD KEY SYMBOLS

COLOURS / SHADES / SHAPES / NUMBERS

NAMES / PEOPLE / BODY PARTS / CHARACTERISTICS

PLACES / TIMES / DATES / POSITIONS

THOUGHTS / FEELINGS / SOUNDS / SMELLS

OBJECTS / ACTIONS / ANIMALS / VEHICLES / FOOD

RECORD UNDERSTANDING

WHAT GOD IS SAYING…

KEY SCRIPTURES:

NOTES.

And it was so, when Gideon heard the telling of the **dream**, and the **interpretation** thereof, that he worshipped, and returned into the host of Israel, and said, Arise; for the Lord hath delivered into your hand the host of Midian.

(JUDGES 7:15)

RECORD YOUR DREAM

DATE: TIME:

INTERPRETATION

Was this dream from God? ☐ Yes ☐ No

(If the dream was not from God, it does not require an interpretation. However, still sit with the Lord to identify the source and to see what He would have you do.)

RECORD KEY SYMBOLS

COLOURS / SHADES / SHAPES / NUMBERS
NAMES / PEOPLE / BODY PARTS / CHARACTERISTICS
PLACES / TIMES / DATES / POSITIONS
THOUGHTS / FEELINGS / SOUNDS / SMELLS
OBJECTS / ACTIONS / ANIMALS / VEHICLES / FOOD

RECORD UNDERSTANDING

WHAT GOD IS SAYING...
KEY SCRIPTURES:

RECORD YOUR DREAM

DATE: TIME:

INTERPRETATION

Was this dream from God? ☐ Yes ☐ No

(If the dream was not from God, it does not require an interpretation. However, still sit with the Lord to identify the source and to see what He would have you do.)

RECORD KEY SYMBOLS

COLOURS / SHADES / SHAPES / NUMBERS
NAMES / PEOPLE / BODY PARTS / CHARACTERISTICS
PLACES / TIMES / DATES / POSITIONS
THOUGHTS / FEELINGS / SOUNDS / SMELLS
OBJECTS / ACTIONS / ANIMALS / VEHICLES / FOOD

RECORD UNDERSTANDING

WHAT GOD IS SAYING…
KEY SCRIPTURES:

RECORD YOUR DREAM

DATE: TIME:

INTERPRETATION

Was this dream from God? ☐ Yes ☐ No

(If the dream was not from God, it does not require an interpretation. However, still sit with the Lord to identify the source and to see what He would have you do.)

RECORD KEY SYMBOLS

COLOURS / SHADES / SHAPES / NUMBERS
NAMES / PEOPLE / BODY PARTS / CHARACTERISTICS
PLACES / TIMES / DATES / POSITIONS
THOUGHTS / FEELINGS / SOUNDS / SMELLS
OBJECTS / ACTIONS / ANIMALS / VEHICLES / FOOD

RECORD UNDERSTANDING

WHAT GOD IS SAYING...
KEY SCRIPTURES:

RECORD YOUR DREAM

DATE: TIME:

INTERPRETATION

Was this dream from God? ☐ Yes ☐ No

(If the dream was not from God, it does not require an interpretation. However, still sit with the Lord to identify the source and to see what He would have you do.)

RECORD KEY SYMBOLS

COLOURS / SHADES / SHAPES / NUMBERS
NAMES / PEOPLE / BODY PARTS / CHARACTERISTICS
PLACES / TIMES / DATES / POSITIONS
THOUGHTS / FEELINGS / SOUNDS / SMELLS
OBJECTS / ACTIONS / ANIMALS / VEHICLES / FOOD

RECORD UNDERSTANDING

WHAT GOD IS SAYING...
KEY SCRIPTURES:

RECORD YOUR DREAM

DATE: TIME:

INTERPRETATION

Was this dream from God? ☐ Yes ☐ No

(If the dream was not from God, it does not require an interpretation. However, still sit with the Lord to identify the source and to see what He would have you do.)

RECORD KEY SYMBOLS

COLOURS / SHADES / SHAPES / NUMBERS
NAMES / PEOPLE / BODY PARTS / CHARACTERISTICS
PLACES / TIMES / DATES / POSITIONS
THOUGHTS / FEELINGS / SOUNDS / SMELLS
OBJECTS / ACTIONS / ANIMALS / VEHICLES / FOOD

RECORD UNDERSTANDING

WHAT GOD IS SAYING...
KEY SCRIPTURES:

RECORD YOUR DREAM

DATE: TIME:

INTERPRETATION

Was this dream from God? ☐ Yes ☐ No

(If the dream was not from God, it does not require an interpretation. However, still sit with the Lord to identify the source and to see what He would have you do.)

RECORD KEY SYMBOLS

COLOURS / SHADES / SHAPES / NUMBERS
NAMES / PEOPLE / BODY PARTS / CHARACTERISTICS
PLACES / TIMES / DATES / POSITIONS
THOUGHTS / FEELINGS / SOUNDS / SMELLS
OBJECTS / ACTIONS / ANIMALS / VEHICLES / FOOD

RECORD UNDERSTANDING

WHAT GOD IS SAYING...
KEY SCRIPTURES:

NOTES.

In Gibeon the Lord appeared to Solomon in a **dream** by night: and God said, Ask what I shall give thee.
(1 KINGS 3:5)

RECORD YOUR DREAM

DATE: TIME:

INTERPRETATION

Was this dream from God? ☐ Yes ☐ No

(If the dream was not from God, it does not require an interpretation. However, still sit with the Lord to identify the source and to see what He would have you do.)

RECORD KEY SYMBOLS

COLOURS / SHADES / SHAPES / NUMBERS
NAMES / PEOPLE / BODY PARTS / CHARACTERISTICS
PLACES / TIMES / DATES / POSITIONS
THOUGHTS / FEELINGS / SOUNDS / SMELLS
OBJECTS / ACTIONS / ANIMALS / VEHICLES / FOOD

RECORD UNDERSTANDING

WHAT GOD IS SAYING...
KEY SCRIPTURES:

RECORD YOUR DREAM

DATE: TIME:

INTERPRETATION

Was this dream from God? ☐ Yes ☐ No

(If the dream was not from God, it does not require an interpretation. However, still sit with the Lord to identify the source and to see what He would have you do.)

RECORD KEY SYMBOLS

COLOURS / SHADES / SHAPES / NUMBERS
NAMES / PEOPLE / BODY PARTS / CHARACTERISTICS
PLACES / TIMES / DATES / POSITIONS
THOUGHTS / FEELINGS / SOUNDS / SMELLS
OBJECTS / ACTIONS / ANIMALS / VEHICLES / FOOD

RECORD UNDERSTANDING

WHAT GOD IS SAYING...
KEY SCRIPTURES:

RECOMMENDED.

Christian Dream Dictionary:

www.pura-t-international.org.uk/christian-dream-dictionary

www.ingramcontent.com/pod-product-compliance
Lightning Source LLC
Chambersburg PA
CBHW080918190726
48293CB00011B/2685
9781999961671